AF715307

Courtroom Control

Narcissistic Wifes, Volume 7

Dr Paul J Peloquin Sr, PhD

Published by Dr Paul J Peloquin Sr, PhD, 2025.

While every precaution has been taken in the preparation of this book, the publisher assumes no responsibility for errors or omissions, or for damages resulting from the use of the information contained herein.

COURTROOM CONTROL

First edition. June 6, 2025.

Copyright © 2025 Dr Paul J Peloquin Sr, PhD.

ISBN: 979-8232226008

Written by Dr Paul J Peloquin Sr, PhD.

Table of Contents

COURTROOM CONTROL

Prologue: When Truth Isn't Enough

By Dr. Paul J. Peloquin, Sr., PhD

I never imagined I'd be sitting in a courtroom, accused of things I didn't do—by a woman I once trusted.

There I was: calm, composed, well-documented, and honest. But none of that seemed to matter. The courtroom didn't feel like a place of justice. It felt like a stage where I was the main course—one where my narcissistic wife played the role of victim so convincingly that even seasoned professionals leaned in, emotionally hooked by her performance.

She cried on cue. She painted me as controlling, abusive, unhinged. Her words were polished lies wrapped in just enough truth to be believable. I watched, helplessly, as her attorney (Which I Paid for FYI) spun the story, and the judge nodded along, oblivious to the subtle, manipulative power play happening in plain sight.

I had evidence. I had character witnesses. I had logic. But what I didn't have was the one thing the court craved more than truth—emotionally persuasive optics.

That day, I learned a brutal truth: the courtroom isn't just a place for facts. It's a battleground where appearances, manipulation, and psychological tactics often win over logic and reality. And narcissists know this. In fact, they thrive in it. I was hammered at every hearing ....

What followed was a relentless legal onslaught—false accusations, emergency motions, manipulated text messages, and an exhausting stream of court dates designed to drain me financially and emotionally. Every hearing felt like a trap. Every ruling a coin toss. I began to question whether the system was broken—or if it was simply blind to this type of calculated abuse.

But I didn't give up.

I studied. I fought back. I learned how narcissists twist the legal system into a weapon—and how to take that weapon away from them.

This book is not just about survival—it's about strategy. It's about exposing the game, understanding the rules, and reclaiming your power in a system that too often overlooks the truth in favor of theatrics.

If you're here, chances are you're in the fight of your life. You're not alone. And you're not crazy. You're standing in the shadow of a master manipulator who knows how to use the courtroom as a stage, a sword, and a shield—all at once.

I wrote this book to help you fight smarter.

Because when truth isn't enough... you need tools.

Let's begin.

— Dr. Paul J. Peloquin, Sr., PhD

Chapter 1: The Narcissist's Legal Playbook

By Dr. Paul J. Peloquin, Sr., PhD

To the outside world, a courtroom is a place for fairness, evidence, and truth. To a narcissist, it's a stage. It's the perfect setting for manipulation, performance, and ultimate control. While most people dread legal battles, narcissists thrive in them—because the courtroom, like their relationships, is a place where illusion can overshadow integrity.

If you're going to survive the narcissist's legal assault, you must first understand their game plan. Because they have one. Make no mistake: everything they do in court is calculated, scripted, and self-serving.

This chapter exposes the inner workings of the narcissist's legal playbook—so you can stop reacting and start preparing.

Narcissists Don't Seek Justice—They Seek Victory

The narcissist doesn't care about fairness. They don't enter court hoping for a balanced outcome. They want control, dominance, and punishment. Their legal strategy is not built around facts—it's built around how things look.

Courtroom battles give narcissists something they crave:

- A stage for sympathy
- An audience of authority figures
- A way to rewrite the story with themselves as the hero—or the victim

When they feel exposed in the relationship, they shift the battleground to court, where their lies can be wrapped in legal paperwork and emotional theatrics.

Behind the Scenes: How Narcissists Plan Their Legal Assault

By the time you receive the first court document, they've already rehearsed their role.

Here's what many narcissists do in the months leading up to the filing:

- Visit multiple attorneys to conflict you out
- Open secret financial accounts or drain joint ones
- Delete or manipulate communication history
- Begin documenting selective incidents that support a distorted narrative
- Start a campaign of subtle provocation to bait you into reactions they can later present as "evidence"

They understand that once they set the narrative, you're on defense—and in family court, the burden of proof is often subjective.

The Core Tactics of the Narcissist's Legal Playbook

1. False Victimhood

Narcissists flip the script instantly: you become the abuser; they become the emotionally scarred survivor.

They may:

- Cry in court, recounting "years of fear"
- Claim psychological damage you supposedly inflicted
- Bring up selective texts or emails, out of context, to paint you as volatile

Their accusations are designed to:

- Preemptively discredit your defense
- Gain temporary legal advantage (custody, protective orders,

property)
- Secure sympathy from judges or evaluators

And because courts often err on the side of caution, they can succeed—at least initially.

2. WEAPONIZED DOCUMENTATION

Narcissists are notorious for selective evidence. They often:

- Present cherry-picked screenshots
- Submit heavily edited conversations
- Introduce "witnesses" who are friends, relatives, or therapists they've manipulated

This isn't an accident. It's a coordinated misinformation campaign dressed in official-looking paperwork.

3. Emergency Motions and Restraining Orders

Nothing moves the court faster than a claim of danger. Narcissists exploit this by filing:

- Ex parte restraining orders
- Emergency custody motions
- Injunctions based on emotional distress or manufactured fear

These filings are rarely about safety—they're about removing you from the home, isolating the children, and gaining immediate leverage.

You may walk into a courtroom to defend yourself, only to find your world has already been reshaped by one signature on a temporary order.

4. Playing the Judge

Narcissists often act differently in front of a judge than they do behind closed doors. They become:

- Respectful, composed, tearful
- Apologetic ("I didn't want this to happen... I just had no choice")
- Almost saint-like in their restraint and dignity

Meanwhile, any hint of frustration or passion from you is painted as evidence of aggression.

This is image control, not emotional truth. And it works—until you expose it with precision.

Courtroom Theater: Understanding Their Psychological Advantage

Narcissists are master performers. In court, they use psychological tricks to gain the upper hand, including:

- Gaslighting through testimony: "He's always been like this, Your Honor."
- Projection: Accusing you of the very things they've done
- Triangulation: Pulling the judge or mediator into a dynamic where you are the aggressor and they are the misunderstood victim
- Smearing you before you arrive: So the court already has doubts about your character

Judges—overloaded with cases and often under-informed about covert narcissism—may fall for the show. This is why documentation, tone control, and preparation are your greatest weapons.

Reader Insight: What One Father Faced

One father shared with me that his ex-wife filed for emergency custody after he refused to change their child's school district—something they had jointly agreed on months earlier. In court, she claimed the child had "severe anxiety" caused by his "rigidity and control."

She cried. She said she was "terrified he'd retaliate." She brought a note from a therapist—one she had coached for months, based only on her word.

He nearly lost temporary custody.

It wasn't until he presented their signed agreement, a recording of their planning conversation, and texts where she praised his involvement that the judge began to see through the act.

He didn't win by being emotional. He won by being prepared.

How to Disarm the Playbook—Without Playing Their Game

Turning the playbook against them doesn't mean sinking to their level. It means rising above it—with evidence, structure, and precision.

Be Impeccably Calm

The narcissist expects you to blow up. Don't. Your self-control is your credibility.

Document Everything

Keep logs, emails, photos, timelines. Use apps that record communication (e.g., TalkingParents, OurFamilyWizard). Your record is your reality.

Argue Their Narrative—Refocus It

Instead of saying "She's lying," say:

> "Here's the email she sent me on March 5. It contradicts what she stated under oath."

Let facts destroy fiction.

Control the Frame

Keep every court appearance centered on the children, the law, and the evidence. Refuse emotional detours.

How This Book Will Equip You

This book will show you how to:

- Recognize legal manipulation early
- Build an airtight documentation system
- Frame your arguments in legal, not emotional, terms
- Communicate with attorneys, evaluators, and judges more effectively
- Counter false allegations with strategic truth

But most importantly, it will help you take your power back.

Because the legal system isn't just a courtroom—it's a labyrinth. One where the narcissist hopes you'll get lost.

But now, you've got a map.

Chapter 2: Divorce by Ambush

By Dr. Paul J. Peloquin, Sr., PhD

You think things are rocky but manageable. Maybe you've been walking on eggshells, enduring emotional whiplash, or wondering if you're the one going crazy. Then one day—often without warning—you're served.

A sheriff's knock. A thick envelope. A moment that changes everything. (Protection Order) (Courtroom Order of Tenn.)

This is how narcissists initiate the legal phase of their abuse. Not with dialogue. Not with honesty. But with an ambush. Because control—not closure—is their endgame.

The Setup Begins Long Before the Papers Arrive

By the time you receive the divorce petition, the narcissist has likely been preparing for months. Here's what they've probably already done behind the scenes:

- Consulted multiple attorneys—not to hire them all, but to conflict you out from using them later.
- Stashed or rerouted money—opening secret accounts, draining joint ones, or claiming they "just forgot" to tell you about new debts.
- Gathered evidence—selectively chosen texts, emails, or even private journal entries to be weaponized later.
- Created a narrative—to present to friends, therapists, attorneys, and eventually the court: You are controlling. You are unstable. You are the problem.

This isn't just divorce. This is a covert war, and you're the last to find out it started.

\Why They Ambush Instead of Confront

Narcissists avoid confrontation unless they control every variable. A direct conversation about divorce would give you time to think, react, or prepare. That's too risky.

Instead, they orchestrate chaos:

- A surprise filing.
- A fabricated emergency.
- A temporary restraining order timed for maximum disruption.

These moves are not emotional outbursts—they're calculated assaults.

The goal? To destabilize you. If they can catch you off guard, they can make you look irrational when you respond.

Common Signs You're Being Set Up

In hindsight, many survivors see clear red flags in the weeks or months before the ambush. Here are some subtle (and not-so-subtle) indicators:

- Sudden sweetness or compliance from your narcissistic spouse—she may be lowering your guard.
- Requests to sign unfamiliar financial documents or make changes to insurance policies.
- Increased accusations, surveillance, or odd questions designed to provoke a reaction.
- Claims that she's seeing a therapist or "just needs space"—often part of image management.
- Disengagement from shared life responsibilities—she's mentally already out.

What Happens in the First 48 Hours

After you're served, the narcissist may strike with a flurry of actions:

- Emergency custody filings
- Restraining orders (often based on fabricated or exaggerated claims)
- Social media smears
- Mass texts or emails to family/friends positioning herself as the victim

The initial legal filing may be filled with shocking allegations—ones you know are false, but ones crafted to gain immediate court sympathy and hand her early control.

You may feel paralyzed. Numb. Furious. But your response in the first few days is critical

How to Respond (Without Playing into Her Hands)

1. Do Not React Emotionally

She wants you to panic, lash out, or go on a crusade to defend yourself publicly. That proves her "abusive" narrative.

Breathe. Respond, don't react.

2. Secure Legal Counsel Immediately

Time is not your friend here. The longer you delay, the more control she seizes.

If she's already spoken to multiple attorneys in your area (to conflict you out), widen your search fast. Consider traveling outside your immediate area to find someone experienced in high-conflict divorce.

3. Collect and Preserve Evidence

Start organizing:

- Texts, emails, voicemails
- Financial statements
- Photos and screenshots
- Witness statements (especially those showing your parenting or character)

Even if her accusations seem outlandish, document everything.

4. Say as Little as Possible

Do not engage in confrontational conversations, and never assume your communications are private. Assume she is recording everything.

5. Protect Your Kids Emotionally

If children are involved, they're likely already being pulled into her narrative. Stay consistent, calm, and safe. Let your actions speak louder than her words.

WHAT THIS ATTACK IS Really About

This isn't about ending a marriage. It's about control, image preservation, and winning—as defined by her ego. A narcissist doesn't just want a divorce; she wants a public exoneration and your quiet humiliation.

By ambushing you legally, she tries to ensure you're too shocked to defend yourself properly. But when you regain your footing and fight strategically—not emotionally—you shift the power dynamic.

What Comes Next

After the ambush comes the second phase of the narcissist's legal warfare: false accusations and protective orders. These tactics are not just disruptive—they are designed to paint you as a threat and solidify her status as the victim in court.

In the next chapter, we'll explore how narcissists exploit restraining orders, exaggerate or fabricate abuse claims, and manipulate the system to gain full control of your reputation, your home, and your children—before you've even said a word in your own defense.

This is war by paperwork. But you don't have to lose it.

Chapter 3: False Accusations and Protective Orders

By Dr. Paul J. Peloquin, Sr., PhD

The courtroom is supposed to be a place where truth rises and justice prevails. But when you're dealing with a narcissist, that ideal can quickly dissolve into a dangerous illusion. One of the most devastating tools in their legal arsenal is the false accusation—particularly when it leads to a protective order that strips you of your rights before you even have a chance to speak.

It starts with a lie. A calculated story. A statement that sounds just plausible enough to stir fear and urgency in the mind of a judge.

Suddenly, you're not a husband or father anymore. You're a threat. And the burden is on you to prove otherwise.

The Strategic Use of False Allegations

Narcissists don't just file claims—they file them with timing, narrative, and emotional manipulation in mind.

False accusations aren't made randomly. They're part of a scripted campaign to:

- Establish immediate control over the home and children
- Gain leverage in custody or financial disputes
- Create a legal and emotional fog around your character

They know that allegations create suspicion, even if they're never proven. In the eyes of the court, where there's smoke, there must be fire. This perception is their greatest weapon.

Common Types of False Accusations

1. Physical Abuse
    - Often vague: "He shoved me" or "He blocked the door."
    - May involve self-inflicted injuries or exaggerated descriptions.
2. Emotional Abuse
    - "He intimidates me," "He's mentally unstable," "I'm afraid of him."
    - Hard to disprove, especially when paired with emotional testimony.
3. Sexual Misconduct
    - Rare, but extremely damaging. Sometimes used when children are involved.
4. Child Neglect or Endangerment
    - "He leaves the kids alone," "He yelled in front of them," "He drinks excessively."
    - Often paired with requests for emergency custody.
5. Stalking or Harassment
    - May include normal contact framed as obsessive behavior: texts, calls, even presence at a shared location.

Why Protective Orders Are So Dangerous

Protective orders—also called restraining orders or injunctions—can be granted without your presence or input. This is called an ex parte order.

Once issued, it can:

- Remove you from your home
- Bar you from seeing your children

- Restrict your access to firearms
- Damage your employment or licensing status
- Be used against you in custody and divorce proceedings

All before you've had a single chance to respond.

It's legal abuse disguised as protection. And for narcissists, it's the ultimate trump card.

How They Pull It Off

To file for a protective order, your narcissistic spouse only needs to appear emotionally distressed and provide a semi-coherent story that sounds credible. Often, they:

- Selectively present evidence (e.g., a single angry text out of context)
- Fabricate timelines to create urgency
- Coach their delivery to appear fragile and terrified
- Use witnesses who are biased or misinformed

Judges, trying to err on the side of caution, often grant temporary orders "just in case."

It's not about proving guilt—it's about presenting risk.

How to Respond If You're Falsely Accused

1. Do Not Retaliate or Contact Her

Even if the allegations are outrageous, do not reach out to her—no calls, texts, emails, or social media contact. Violating the order—even unintentionally—can result in criminal charges.

2. Hire a Lawyer with Experience in False Allegations

Not all attorneys understand the narcissistic dynamic. You need one who can:

- Challenge credibility
- Expose contradictions
- Present your emotional restraint as strength

3. Collect Evidence Immediately

- Full communication records (texts, emails, voicemails)
- GPS data, receipts, phone logs (to prove location)
- Witness statements or surveillance if available
- Evidence of prior threats or manipulations

4. Stay Calm in Court

Your calmness will be interpreted as credibility. Her theatrics will be noted by the judge—if you remain composed and fact-focused.

5. Request a Full Hearing

If the order was granted ex parte, demand a hearing. At that hearing:

- Present hard evidence
- Avoid emotional outbursts
- Demonstrate logic and restraint

Exposing the Pattern Over Time

One false claim can ruin your reputation. But a pattern of manipulative behavior is harder for the court to ignore—especially if you document it over time.

Create a timeline of her behavior:

- Dates of controlling or erratic actions
- Financial manipulations
- Parental alienation efforts
- Emotional volatility or threats

This becomes part of your credibility portfolio. You may not win sympathy, but you can win respect.

A Word on Law Enforcement

Many men are shocked when police enforce a restraining order without investigation. That's because it's a civil order, and the police aren't there to evaluate truth—they're there to enforce compliance.

Stay calm, obey the order fully, and take the fight to court—not the street.

Psychological Toll of Being Accused

Being falsely labeled an abuser can shatter your self-image. You may feel:

- Humiliated
- Disbelieved
- Isolated
- Powerless

That's exactly what she wants.

Understand: this isn't about who you are. It's about the role she needs you to play to validate her victimhood. You don't have to play it. You can choose truth over theater.

Coming Next: Custody Warfare

When a narcissist begins using your children as legal leverage, the damage deepens—for both you and the kids. In the next chapter, we'll look at the fatherhood trap, how courts are often blind to parental alienation, and what you can do to protect your relationship with your children before it's too late.

This is where the real war begins.

Chapter 4: Custody Battles and the Fatherhood Trap

By Dr. Paul J. Peloquin, Sr., PhD

If there's one weapon more powerful than false accusations, it's the threat of losing your children.

Narcissists understand that a father's love is his greatest vulnerability. They know that if they can control the narrative around custody, they control you—emotionally, legally, and financially. And once that control is cemented in a courtroom, undoing it is a slow, uphill battle.

They don't just want custody. They want ownership of the story—one where you are painted as dangerous, unreliable, or "unfit." Even if you've been a consistent, loving parent for years, that history is rewritten overnight.

And suddenly, the person weaponizing the legal system isn't just coming after your reputation. They're coming after your bond with your children.

The Narcissist's Custody Strategy

Narcissists view children as tools, not people. In custody disputes, this translates into three primary tactics:

1. The "Protective Mother" Persona

She will appear in court as nurturing, concerned, and self-sacrificing—even if she's emotionally neglectful at home. She plays the martyr, often claiming:

- "He's too aggressive."
- "The kids are scared of him."

- "I've always been the primary caregiver."

Even if these statements are completely false, they feed the court's tendency to default to maternal preference.

2. Parental Alienation

Behind the scenes, she poisons the children's perception of you through:

- Subtle criticism ("Your dad only cares about himself.")
- Emotional bribery ("If you love me, don't go with him.")
- Creating fear or confusion ("He might get angry if you say that.")

Over time, the children may begin to reject you—not because of anything you did, but because they're trying to survive emotional pressure.

3. Custody as Leverage

She may use custody as a bargaining chip in financial negotiations:

- "I'll agree to joint custody if you give up the house."
- "I won't ask for child support if you agree to supervised visitation."

To her, your relationship with your kids is a currency to be spent.

The Court's Blind Spot

Family courts often operate under the assumption that both parents are flawed but well-meaning. Judges want to avoid disruption and maintain peace, especially for the children's sake.

This is where the narcissist thrives. They know how to:

- Weaponize the language of concern and safety
- Present themselves as cooperative while subtly sabotaging your rights

- Exploit the court's bias toward mothers, especially in younger children

Courts may misread your calmness as detachment and her hysteria as maternal instinct. Unless you document and expose her manipulations, the system will default to the path of least resistance—and that often favors the narcissist.

How to Protect Yourself and Your Children

1. Document Everything

Keep a detailed parenting journal. Note:

- Missed exchanges
- Negative statements made to the children
- Changes in your child's behavior after visits
- Any refusal of communication or access

Use timestamps, screenshots, emails—facts, not feelings.

2. Insist on Written Agreements

Never trust verbal parenting plans. Narcissists rarely honor them.

- Insist on a formal, court-ordered parenting schedule
- Communicate only through text or email when possible

3. Stay Consistent

Children need emotional stability. The narcissist may manipulate them, but they will remember who showed up—consistently, calmly, and lovingly. Over time, your presence can rebuild trust, even if alienation has taken root.

4. Consider a Guardian ad Litem (GAL)

In complex cases, request that the court appoint a GAL or parenting evaluator. This person can investigate the situation and make recommendations. While not perfect, it can introduce a third party to challenge the narcissist's narrative.

5. Beware of "Disney Parenting"

Narcissists often avoid rules and discipline during their parenting time. This makes you look like "the strict one" while they buy loyalty with gifts, junk food, or leniency.

Don't try to compete—stay grounded in your values. Over time, kids crave safety over fun.

WHEN THEY TRY TO CUT You Out Completely

Some narcissists attempt the nuclear option: full custody and total removal of your parenting rights. They'll justify it with dramatic claims:

- "He's emotionally unstable."
- "He's never around."
- "He just wants control."

If this happens:

- File a motion for shared custody immediately
- Provide character references and parenting logs
- Don't wait for the court to see through her—make it undeniable

You are not just fighting for visitation. You're fighting for your children's right to know you, trust you, and be protected from emotional manipulation.

Long-Term Impact on the Children

Children raised by narcissistic mothers often develop:

- Anxiety, people-pleasing tendencies
- Fear of expressing needs
- Confusion around boundaries
- Guilt for loving both parents

You may not be able to shield them from all harm. But you can be the lighthouse that helps them navigate the storm.

Even if they pull away now, many children return later—grateful that one parent never gave up on them.

Coming Next: The Court's Blind Spot

Why do so many judges miss these manipulations? Why do they misread calm fathers as indifferent and narcissistic mothers as "concerned caregivers"? In the next chapter, I-will expose and examine how the legal system's good intentions can be used as blind spots—and how you can use logic, evidence, and precision to guide the court back to the truth.

Chapter 5: The Court's Blind Spot

By Dr. Paul J. Peloquin, Sr., PhD

The courtroom is built on the premise that truth will prevail—but that premise collapses when manipulation goes unnoticed and unchecked. Family court, in particular, was designed with good intentions: to protect children, promote fairness, and resolve conflict. But for all its structure and legal formality, it remains deeply human. And that's exactly where the danger lies when a narcissist steps into the arena.

Narcissists exploit the blind spots of human perception. And unfortunately, judges, mediators, attorneys, and custody evaluators are just as susceptible to their illusions as anyone else—sometimes even more so.

Why the System Often Gets It Wrong

Judges are trained in law—not in psychological manipulation. They rely on:

- Emotional presentation
- Historical gender roles
- Legal evidence
- Assumptions of rationality

When a narcissist walks into court weeping, shaking, and using trigger words like "afraid," "abuse," or "coercive control," the system reacts quickly—and often without verification. On the surface, she appears fragile and sincere. You, by contrast, may appear calm, restrained, or even frustrated—traits that can be misread as coldness or guilt.

That's the paradox of being a male victim: the more dignified you are, the more suspicious you may appear.

COMMON JUDICIAL MISINTERPRETATIONS

1. Calm Equals Uncaring
    - Judges expect emotional testimony. When a man stays calm and collected, it can seem robotic or insincere.
    - In reality, you may be holding yourself together with every ounce of strength—because you know the courtroom is not a place for outbursts.
2. Tears Equal Truth
    - Narcissists are skilled at crying on command, showing vulnerability, and using emotional phrasing.
    - Judges may interpret this as evidence of trauma rather than performance.
3. Mother = Default Nurturer
    - Despite modern reforms, many courts still hold subconscious biases favoring maternal custody, especially with young children.
4. Control Claims
    - A narcissist may accuse you of "controlling" her—when in truth, you were trying to protect the family, manage finances, or respond to erratic behavior.
    - These accusations are rarely challenged unless you bring objective, timeline-based evidence.

The System Favors Stability—Not Always Justice

Family court prioritizes:

- Finality
- Peace
- Structure

So when judges see two people in conflict, they don't necessarily look for truth. They look for the easiest path forward. And narcissists excel at appearing cooperative while painting you as rigid, unreasonable, or emotionally flat.

You may hear phrases like:

- "Let's just move forward."
- "We're not here to litigate the past."
- "Both parties need to be more flexible."

This is maddening. Especially when the past is exactly what's shaping the present abuse.

HOW TO HELP THE COURT See What It Misses

The key to exposing narcissistic manipulation isn't emotion—it's precision.

1. Present Patterns, Not Just Incidents

Instead of saying "She lied about X," show a pattern of behavior:

- A timeline of false claims
- Inconsistent statements in emails and court filings
- Examples of manipulative parenting

Judges respond to structure more than story.

2. Avoid Diagnosing Her in Court

Never say "She's a narcissist." Judges aren't therapists, and this sounds like finger-pointing.

Instead, describe the behavior:

- "She routinely withholds the children when upset."
- "She makes unilateral decisions and denies communication."
- "She has filed five motions in six months, all of which were dismissed."

Let the court conclude her instability on its own.

3. Use Legal Language, Not Emotional Language

Don't say:

- "She's toxic."
- "She ruined my life."
- "She's brainwashing the kids."

Do say:

- "There's a sustained pattern of interference with court-ordered visitation."
- "The child is expressing language that seems coached or rehearsed."
- "She made unsubstantiated abuse claims immediately after I filed for custody."

THIS DEMONSTRATES CREDIBILITY and control.

4. Bring Witnesses—Carefully

Third-party witnesses can help, especially professionals:

- Therapists
- Teachers
- Babysitters
- Coaches

Avoid mutual friends or family unless their neutrality is unquestionable.

When the Court Still Doesn't Get It

Sometimes, even airtight evidence is ignored or dismissed. If that happens:

- File appeals when necessary—but only with strong legal grounds
- Stay consistent in parenting—children are watching more than the judge
- Build long-term credibility—courts may reverse decisions when patterns emerge over time

Don't self-destruct. The narcissist wants you to explode, quit, or spiral. That reaction validates everything she's said. Your restraint is your advantage, even if it doesn't feel like it in the moment.

The Hard Truth

You are not guaranteed fairness. But you can command respect by being relentless with facts, firm in your presence, and strategic in your advocacy.

It may take multiple hearings. It may take appeals. But courts eventually respond to evidence of patterns. When you demonstrate consistency, while the narcissist's lies slowly unravel, the tide begins to shift.

Justice delayed does not have to mean justice denied.

Coming Next: Building Your Legal Armor

The courtroom is a battlefield. You need more than truth—you need strategy. In the next chapter, we'll cover how to choose the right lawyer, document like a professional, and develop the mindset and tools to withstand even the most vicious legal onslaught.

You're not just defending yourself. You're protecting your future.

Chapter 6: Building Your Legal Armor

By Dr. Paul J. Peloquin, Sr., PhD

Walking into court without a strategy when facing a narcissist is like walking into a gunfight with your hands in your pockets. They've been preparing long before you realized there was a war. If you're going to survive—and win—you need more than the truth. You need legal armor.

This chapter is your blueprint for preparing mentally, emotionally, and practically for what's ahead.

1. The Right Attorney: Your Shield and Sword

Not all attorneys are equipped to deal with narcissistic abuse. Many are trained for negotiation, not psychological warfare. You need one who:

- Understands high-conflict personalities
- Has experience with false accusations and custody battles
- Is responsive, not dismissive
- Thinks strategically, not just procedurally

Interview your attorney like your freedom depends on it—because it does.

Ask:

- "How do you handle clients facing false accusations?"
- "What's your experience with custody involving parental alienation?"

- "How aggressive are you willing to be when needed?"

If they downplay your concerns or suggest you "just cooperate" with outrageous demands, keep looking. You need an advocate—not a referee.

2. Document Like a Prosecutor

In a narcissist's legal assault, evidence is your weapon. Courts believe documentation over recollection.

Set up a system:

- Create folders: one for each issue—custody, finances, communication, etc.
- Use timelines: Record when events happen, what was said, and who was present.
- Print everything: Emails, texts, social media posts, Venmo logs—anything that tells the story.
- Back it up: Cloud storage + external hard drive + USB. Assume she'll delete or sabotage anything she can.

Even screenshots of deleted messages matter. Courts respect facts they can see.

3. Master Communication Control

A narcissist thrives on emotional chaos—especially over text and email. Your job is to remove the fuel.

Use BIFF:

Brief, Informative, Friendly, Firm

Example:

Bad: "You're lying again and you know it. You always twist the truth."

Good: "Per our parenting agreement, I'll pick up the children at 3 PM. Let me know if there's a conflict."

THIS APPROACH:

- Keeps you calm
- Builds a record of professionalism
- Destroys their narrative of you being aggressive or unhinged

Use apps like:

- OurFamilyWizard
- TalkingParents

These tools are court-admissible and limit manipulation.

4. Strengthen Your Mental Resilience

Legal battles with narcissists are marathons, not sprints. You will be tested—over months or even years.

To maintain your composure:

- Therapy or coaching: Preferably with someone who understands narcissistic abuse
- Meditation or journaling: To release internal stress without external fallout
- Fitness and routine: Physical discipline reinforces emotional strength
- Limit contact: Block her where you can; engage only when legally necessary

This is war. You must protect your mind as much as your rights.

5. Build Your Credibility Portfolio

Start crafting a case that goes beyond defense. Show the judge who you really are:

- Photos with your children
- Letters from teachers, neighbors, coworkers
- Consistent child support payments
- Volunteering, community involvement
- Clean background and work history

This builds a story of stability, reliability, and good character—the opposite of the picture she's trying to paint.

6. Fall for Her Legal Traps

A narcissist will:

- Bait you into angry texts to use in court
- Cry abuse when she's the one being abusive
- Drag out proceedings to drain your finances and energy

Every move you make must be measured, documented, and focused on the outcome. Don't argue to be "right." Argue to win custody. Argue to keep your assets. Argue to regain peace.

7. Monitor Financial Warfare

Many narcissists use money to punish. Be ready to counter:

- Hidden accounts
- Secret spending
- Frozen joint funds
- Unauthorized debts

Get copies of:

- Bank statements (at least 12–24 months)

- Tax returns
- Credit reports
- Insurance policies

Hire a forensic accountant if large sums or business income are involved. Courts respect hard numbers more than personal pleas.

8. Understand the System—and Outsmart It

- Motions: File when she breaks orders—don't wait.
- Depositions: Prepare her contradictions ahead of time.
- Court appearances: Dress professionally, speak calmly, focus on children if involved.
- Mediation: Be cautious. Don't agree to terms just to end the process. What you sign, you must live with.

Your strategy should be structured, not reactive. Let her spiral while you stay the course.

When the System Seems Against You

Even with preparation, the court may initially believe her. That doesn't mean you've lost.

What wins cases is consistency.

- Show up.
- Stay calm.
- Present facts.
- Never give up.

The narcissist will overplay her hand eventually. She'll lie too obviously. Contradict herself. Sabotage her own credibility.

When she does, you'll be ready—with armor forged in truth, strategy, and unwavering discipline.

Coming Next: Narcissists in Mediation

You might be told that mediation is the best option—but when dealing with a narcissist, mediation can become another stage for control, deception, and manipulation. In the next chapter, you'll learn how to spot the traps, maintain leverage, and walk away with your dignity—and your goals—intact.

Chapter 7: Narcissists in Mediation

By Dr. Paul J. Peloquin, Sr., PhD

At first glance, mediation seems like a safe haven in a turbulent divorce. A place where two adults can avoid the chaos of court, save money, and find common ground. That's the theory.

But if one of those adults is a narcissist, mediation becomes anything but fair. Instead of being a forum for peace, it becomes a breeding ground for deception, manipulation, and psychological pressure.

For a narcissist, mediation is a stage—quiet, private, and free from the strict rules of the courtroom. And unlike a judge, mediators aren't there to render justice. They're there to guide compromise. This is why narcissists love it.

Because compromise, to them, means you surrender.

The Real Purpose of Mediation (And Why It Fails with Narcissists)

Mediation is meant to:

- Reduce court time
- Foster collaborative solutions
- Help parents or spouses resolve differences with civility
- Protect children from legal warfare

It only works when both parties operate in good faith.

That doesn't happen when one party is emotionally dishonest, pathologically self-centered, and obsessed with control. The narcissist doesn't walk into mediation looking for fairness. She walks in looking for a power imbalance she can exploit.=

She knows there's no judge to object to emotional manipulation. She knows the mediator wants resolution more than justice. She knows you're tired, emotionally drained, and possibly still healing from her abuse.

How Narcissists Manipulate Mediation

1. Image Management in Full Effect

In mediation, narcissists turn up the charm. They smile, cry at the right moments, and make subtle jabs that appear innocent to the untrained eye.

They say things like:

- "I'm really just trying to keep things stable for the children."
- "He gets so angry—I'm scared he might snap."
- "I'm willing to give up so much... I just want peace."

These phrases are designed to:

- Make you look unreasonable if you disagree
- Win sympathy from the mediator
- Exert pressure to accept unfavorable terms

And because most mediators are not trauma-informed or trained in narcissistic behavior, they may buy into this performance.

2. Emotional Blackmail Behind Closed Doors

When the mediator steps out—or during breaks—the narcissist may confront you with:

- "If you fight this, I'll make sure the kids resent you."
- "I'll take everything you have if you don't give me what I want."
- "Just sign it. Don't drag this out any longer."

These are scare tactics meant to wear you down. They want you to cave—not because the agreement is fair, but because you're exhausted and confused.

3. The "Fair but Fatal" Offer

Narcissists are skilled at proposing settlements that appear reasonable but are actually traps.

For example:

> "We'll do 50/50 custody—but I get full legal decision-making because I'm more available."

That sounds balanced. Until you realize it gives her the power to choose schools, deny therapy, refuse medical decisions, or relocate without your consent

4. Deliberate Stalling

Sometimes the narcissist drags mediation out—not to resolve anything, but to:

- Buy time to plan her next legal move
- Drain your finances
- Appear "cooperative" to the judge ("See? I tried mediation!")

She has no intention of settling. She just wants to delay the inevitable and wear you down.

Case Example: The "Peacemaker" Trap

One father I worked with was promised shared parenting if he "just agreed to let her have the house." She framed it as:

> "The kids need stability. I'm not trying to hurt you. This is just best for them."

She smiled warmly during mediation, even offered to split holidays evenly.

He agreed.

Two weeks later, she filed a motion for full custody and a restraining order, claiming she "felt unsafe" in the house—even though he had already vacated. She used the mediated agreement as leverage to isolate him from his children.

This is why nothing should be agreed to on emotion alone.

How to Protect Yourself During Mediation

1. Bring an Attorney—Or Keep One on Call

Even if you don't want to litigate, having a legal mind at the table changes everything. Narcissists are less bold when someone else is watching. If you can't afford full representation, hire a lawyer to review any proposed agreement before you sign it.

2. Know Your Non-Negotiables

Before mediation:

- Write down your bottom line for custody, finances, visitation, etc.
- Decide where you can compromise—and where you won't.
- Stick to your list, even if pressured.

Don't "trade" your child's best interests just to end the meeting sooner.

3. Say Little, Document Much

Narcissists bait you into emotional reactions. Don't take the bait.

- Keep your tone neutral.
- Redirect attacks: "Let's stay focused on the parenting schedule."
- Bring a notebook. Take notes on her statements, the mediator's reactions, and anything unusual.

These records may become important if you return to court.

4. Demand Specific Language in the Agreement

Vague agreements are the narcissist's dream.

Bad: "Each parent will be respectful and cooperative."

Good: "Each parent will communicate through TalkingParents. Visitation exchanges occur at 6:00 PM every Friday at the police station parking lot."

Narcissists exploit ambiguity. Close every loophole.

5. TAKE YOUR TIME—DON'T Sign Immediately

If pressured to sign on the spot, respond with:

> "I'd like to review this with my attorney. I'll get back to you within 48 hours."

You have that right. Don't let fatigue or guilt make permanent decisions.

When to Walk Away from Mediation

Sometimes, refusing to settle is the wisest move. Mediation is not mandatory if it endangers your parental rights or finances.

If you experience:

- Emotional bullying
- One-sided proposals
- Hostile threats masked as "negotiation"

...you can (and should) walk away.

Document your concerns and explain to the court that mediation failed due to bad-faith participation. Judges will often appreciate that you tried before escalating.

WHAT IF YOU'RE FORCED Back into Mediation?

In some jurisdictions, judges will order repeat mediation. If that happens:

- Request a different mediator if bias was present.
- Ask for sessions to be recorded or supervised.
- Stick to your documentation strategy and reinforce your previous terms.

You are allowed to defend yourself—calmly, firmly, legally.

Final Thoughts: Mediation is Just Another Battleground

When you're dealing with a narcissist, mediation is not a shortcut to peace. It's another performance stage. The key difference is—you now know the script.

You understand their tactics. You've prepared your evidence. You know what matters and what doesn't. And most importantly, you've committed to not surrendering under pressure.

You can't change who she is.

But you can control how you respond, what you agree to, and what kind of future you allow her to shape for you and your children.

That's not just surviving mediation. That's winning it.

Chapter 8: Going Pro Se: Representing Yourself with Confidence

By Dr. Paul J. Peloquin, Sr., PhD

Sometimes, the battle lines are drawn without your consent. You may find yourself without legal representation—either by choice, by financial constraint, or because you've been boxed out by the narcissist's tactics. Many men in family court are forced to represent themselves, or go pro se.

That can feel overwhelming. But it doesn't have to mean defeat.

If you're prepared, disciplined, and strategic, you can still protect yourself—and win.

This chapter will teach you how to speak the court's language, carry yourself with authority, and dismantle the narcissist's lies even when you're standing alone.

When Going Pro Se Makes Sense

Going pro se is not always ideal, but in some cases, it may be:

- Necessary (due to financial constraints or legal disqualification)
- Tactical (if your attorney is weak, dismissive, or uninformed about narcissistic abuse)
- Empowering (when you know your case inside and out and are ready to take charge)

Contrary to popular belief, judges do not automatically punish pro se litigants. In fact, some judges may respect your effort if you're prepared, polite, and organized.

What You MUST Understand About the Courtroom

1. The Courtroom is a Stage—Not a Therapy Session

You're not there to vent. You're there to present facts, law, and logic. Keep emotions low, focus tight, and statements brief.

2. Judges Value Structure Over Story

It doesn't matter how painful your experience was if you can't link it to a legal violation. Judges want:

- Specific dates and times
- Documentation
- Breaches of court orders or agreements
- Relevance to the case at hand

3. Your Demeanor is Evidence

The court observes your body language, tone, composure, and attitude as closely as your documents. Calm, respectful behavior builds credibility—even if you don't know every law.

Step-by-Step: How to Represent Yourself Effectively

Step 1: Know the Law and Procedure

- Visit your local court website and download the family court rules
- Learn how to:
    - File a motion
    - Respond to filings
    - Serve the other party
    - Introduce evidence

Don't assume you'll "figure it out in the moment." Practice is power.

Step 2: Organize Your Case File

Create labeled folders:

- Custody
- Communication
- Financials
- Court Orders
- Motions and Responses

Have:

- A printed timeline of events
- A 1-page summary of your requested outcomes
- Extra copies of everything for the judge and the other party

Treat this like a presentation. If your papers are scattered, your case will be, too.

Step 3: Prepare Your Statements

Don't wing it. Write your opening remarks, responses to likely accusations, and your closing summary in advance.

EXAMPLE OPENING:

> "Your Honor, I'm here seeking joint physical custody of my children. I've consistently been involved in their lives, provided financial support, and maintained a safe, loving environment. I've brought documentation to support these facts."

Don't attack. Don't ramble. Be concise and child-focused.

Step 4: Bring Evidence That Speaks for You

Courts love documents. Bring:

- Visitation logs
- Emails/texts (printed, highlighted)
- Photos or school reports
- Missed pickup records
- Proof of compliance with all orders

Let the paperwork do the talking. It's far more persuasive than your opinion.

Step 5: Practice, Practice, Practice

Stand in front of a mirror. Practice responding to:

- "Why do you want custody?"
- "What concerns do you have about the other parent?"
- "Why should the court rule in your favor?"

Record yourself. Watch your tone. Refine your responses.

Avoid These Common Mistakes

- Getting emotional: Anger, sarcasm, or tears undermine your argument.
- Interrupting the judge or the other party: Let them hang themselves with their words. Then respond with grace.
- Bringing irrelevant information: The judge doesn't care about your heartbreak. Focus on legal violations, parenting patterns, and specific harm.
- Failing to object: If the narcissist lies or introduces hearsay, say calmly:

> "Objection, Your Honor. That's not accurate and not supported by the evidence."

Dealing With Her Attorney

If the narcissist has a lawyer:

- Be respectful but firm.
- Don't let them rattle you. Lawyers will often provoke to fluster you.
- Stick to facts. Say:

> "I disagree. Here's the document that proves otherwise."

You do not need to match their legalese. You need to be clear, credible, and consistent.

What the Judge is Looking For

You might think the narcissist's performance is winning—but judges look for:

- Consistency
- Preparedness
- Self-control
- Prioritization of the children

EVERY TIME YOU SPEAK, ask yourself:

> "Does this help the judge understand what's best for the kids?"
>
> "Does this make me look credible and focused?"

The Power of Self-Representation

Representing yourself—successfully—is one of the most empowering things you can do. It tells the court, the narcissist, and more importantly, yourself, that you refuse to be silenced, manipulated, or broken.

You are your own advocate. And when you speak truth with clarity and control, even the most polished lie begins to crack.

Coming Next: Post-Divorce Sabotage

Winning the case doesn't always end the conflict. Narcissists often continue their campaign through noncompliance, co-parenting sabotage, and ongoing legal harassment. In the next chapter, we'll explore how to defend your peace and enforce your rights after the gavel drops.

Chapter 9: Post-Divorce Sabotage

By Dr. Paul J. Peloquin, Sr., PhD

The judge's gavel may bring a ruling, but it rarely brings peace—especially when you're divorcing a narcissist. For most people, divorce marks the beginning of emotional closure. For a narcissist, it's simply the start of a new campaign of control.

This is the phase that catches many men off guard. You survived the accusations. You navigated the courtroom. You even secured fair custody or kept your assets intact. But now, post-divorce, the real warfare begins—through noncompliance, co-parenting sabotage, and ongoing legal harassment.

You are no longer her husband—but in her mind, you are still her property. And if she can't control you through love or marriage, she'll try to do it through fear and frustration.

The Narcissist's Post-Divorce Toolkit

1. Violating Court Orders (Subtly)
    - Withholding the kids for "legitimate" reasons
    - Denying scheduled calls or visitations
    - "Forgetting" to share school or medical information
    - Passive-aggressive lateness or schedule changes
2. Co-Parenting Manipulation
    - Coaching children to mistrust or criticize you
    - Undermining your rules ("You don't have to do that at Mom's")
    - Using your kids as messengers or emotional pawns

3. False Accusations—Again
    - Claiming you violated orders
    - Accusing you of child neglect or abuse without basis
    - Threatening to "take you back to court" repeatedly
4. Ongoing Financial Sabotage
    - Failing to follow child support agreements
    - Racking up joint debts that you thought were closed
    - Filing fraudulent claims or misusing tax credits
5. Smear Campaigns
    - Talking badly about you to friends, teachers, or even on social media
    - Making you appear unstable or dangerous—long after the divorce is final

Why She Keeps the War Alive

The narcissist doesn't seek peace—she seeks power. Even after the marriage is dissolved, she:

- Misses the control she once had
- Fears losing relevance
- Hates that you survived her

To her, your ability to move on is a threat. Your happiness, new relationships, or emotional freedom feel like betrayal. So she attacks again—not with love bombs, but with slow, calculated sabotage.

How to Fight Back Strategically

1. Enforce the Order Relentlessly

The court order is not a suggestion—it's law. Treat it that way.

- Log every violation (missed exchanges, denied calls, etc.)
- Keep a detailed parenting journal with dates, times, and behaviors

- File for contempt when necessary

You may feel tempted to "let it go"—but doing so teaches her she can ignore the system.

2. Communicate in Writing Only

- Use apps like OurFamilyWizard or TalkingParents
- Avoid phone calls unless legally required
- Never respond emotionally—respond factually and briefly

If she sends a rage-filled email accusing you of being "a terrible father," reply:

> "I'll be at the pickup location at 3:00 PM as scheduled. Let me know if there's a delay."

Keep every message. It's your insurance policy.

3. Defend Your Relationship with the Children

- Remain consistent, warm, and emotionally safe—even when the kids pull away
- Avoid badmouthing their mother—this backfires long-term
- Encourage open conversation without pressure or guilt

Your children may be confused, angry, or withdrawn. But deep down, they remember who showed up, who stayed calm, and who loved them without conditions.

4. Set Firm Boundaries

You do not owe your ex:

- Explanations for your private life
- Emotional availability
- Access beyond what's legally required

If she tries to control through guilt or neediness, hold the line. Boundaries are not cruelty—they're survival.

When Legal Harassment Returns

Some narcissists will reopen the legal battle again and again:

- Modifying custody agreements without reason
- Filing false police reports
- Accusing you of contempt to drain your resources

If this happens:

- Ask the court for a litigation gatekeeper or vexatious litigant designation
- Demand she provide evidence before hearings are granted
- Keep records of every dismissed or baseless filing

The court can eventually recognize this abuse of the system. But it's up to you to document the pattern.

HEALING WHILE UNDER Attack

You can still recover, even while she throws grenades from a distance. The key is separating her chaos from your identity.

- Stay in therapy or support groups
- Journal your emotional growth, not just her attacks
- Build a post-divorce life that is stable, quiet, and fulfilling
- Surround yourself with people who validate your truth—not her version of it

You may not be able to control her behavior. But you can control your response, your narrative, and your future.

Coming Next: Turning the Tables

You've survived the storm. Now it's time to reclaim your power. In the final chapter, you'll learn how to document long-term abuse, expose false narratives, and—when the time is right—hold a narcissist legally accountable through countersuits, complaints, and bold truth-telling.

Chapter 10: Turning the Tables

By Dr. Paul J. Peloquin, Sr., PhD

There comes a moment in every battle when the tide begins to shift—not because the opponent has weakened, but because you have grown stronger. That moment is where this chapter begins.

You've been dragged through false accusations, legal traps, custody games, and relentless psychological warfare. You've been underestimated, misrepresented, and silenced. But now, you're still standing—with truth on your side, scars that speak, and a strategy forged in fire.

This is what it means to turn the tables.

And while it may not come with a dramatic courtroom moment or the narcissist's long-overdue confession, it will come with something even more powerful: freedom, clarity, and justice—on your terms.

What "Turning the Tables" Really Means

It's not about revenge. It's about balance.

It means:

- Exposing the narcissist's lies calmly, with documented precision
- Enforcing legal consequences without emotional bait
- Reclaiming your reputation and emotional strength
- Refusing to play the role she cast for you
- Protecting your children and future from repeated abuse

Turning the tables isn't loud. It's deliberate. Quiet power. Tactical thinking. Legal strategy backed by unshakable emotional control.

1. Use Her Patterns Against Her

Narcissists are creatures of habit. Over time, their lies create contradictions. Their smear campaigns lose traction. And their manipulations begin to show cracks—especially when you consistently document the truth.

You must:

- Track every instance of parental interference, false accusation, and court violation
- Create a composite timeline that demonstrates a pattern—not just isolated events
- Present this pattern in future court hearings, custody reviews, or even civil actions

Judges don't act on stories—they act on structure.

The narcissist may fool people once. But when her behavior is recorded and repeated, it becomes her undoing.

---

2. File Strategic Motions and Complaints

You're no longer playing defense. Now, you use the same system she abused—to hold her accountable.

Contempt of Court

If she violates:

- Custody exchanges
- Communication guidelines
- Child support orders

...you file for contempt.

Judges can:

- Fine her

- Order makeup parenting time
- Alter custody permanently
- In rare cases, issue jail time

Contempt motions show that you respect the law—even when she doesn't.

Request Court-Appointed Professionals

- Guardian ad Litem
- Parenting Coordinator
- Custody Evaluator

These third parties can help reveal her instability. Make sure they're trauma-informed and receive documentation before interviews begin.

File for Modification

If her behavior escalates, request modifications:

- Adjust custody from 50/50 to primary
- Request supervised visitation
- Restrict relocation

Turning the tables means reclaiming rights she hoped to strip from you.

3. Expose Her Through Civil Remedies

If the narcissist's behavior was not just manipulative—but malicious—you may have grounds to sue her in civil court. (Which I am Doing)

Consider actions for:

- Defamation: Public lies that damaged your reputation
- Malicious Prosecution: False criminal complaints or injunctions
- Intentional Infliction of Emotional Distress: Especially when

tied to parental alienation
- Fraud: Hidden assets, falsified tax returns, financial lies during discovery

These cases are complex, but you only need one strong victory to change the narrative—and send a message that you're not afraid to fight back legally.

4. File Official Complaints Against Professionals

If her attorney knowingly presented lies...
If her therapist wrote false letters based solely on her word...
If a court-appointed evaluator ignored glaring red flags...
You can and should report them.

- File complaints with the Bar Association for unethical legal conduct
- Report therapists to the Board of Psychology
- Challenge guardian ad litem reports with affidavits and counter-evidence

These systems depend on accountability. And when narcissists use professionals as weapons, your silence protects the abuse.

You don't have to shout. You just have to file.

5. Reclaim Your Public Identity

Narcissists often win the social war, at least temporarily. They isolate you from mutual friends. They tell family you're "unstable." They twist facts and tell only the parts of the story that paint them as the hero.

Turning the tables means reclaiming your voice:

- Begin telling your full story—to safe people first, then trusted circles
- Share your truth with your children in age-appropriate ways when the time is right

- Consider speaking, coaching, or even writing—because your survival matters to others
- Join communities of other male survivors; help them navigate what you just endured

Silence protects her. Storytelling liberates you.

6. Defend and Rebuild the Father-Child Relationship

Turning the tables isn't just about court wins—it's about healing your legacy.

If she's alienated the children, stay steady:

- Send letters, even if they're never answered
- Show up to games or events, even if you sit alone
- Honor the parenting schedule, even when she doesn't
- Keep your door open without guilt, shame, or pressure

Children alienated by narcissistic parents often return in adulthood—if they remember who was safe.

Be that parent.

7. Create a Post-Abuse Life So Stable She Can't Touch It

The final phase of turning the tables is living a life she can no longer disrupt.

- Pay off debts
- Restore your credit
- Build new traditions with your children
- Date again—on your timeline
- Start the business, change the job, reclaim the joy

If she hears about you, let her hear nothing but peace.

If she sees you in court again, let her see a man unshaken.

CASE STUDY: FROM DEFEATED to Determined

One man I counseled lost everything in his first court battle: primary custody, access to his kids, and most of his assets. His wife claimed abuse, staged photos, and cried convincingly in court.

At first, he folded.

But over the next two years, he:

- Documented every missed exchange and lie
- Filed contempt motions with timestamps and video
- Recorded school violations and parental alienation
- Sued her for defamation after her claims were dismissed

He now has primary custody, restored credibility, and is mentoring other men in similar battles.

Not because he fought harder. But because he fought smarter.

8. Redefine Victory

Victory doesn't always look like a courtroom reversal. Sometimes it looks like:

- Peaceful time with your kids
- Financial stability after years of chaos
- The ability to sleep without fear
- Walking away from her bait with nothing but silence

You've turned the tables when:

- You no longer respond to her manipulations
- You no longer fear her next move
- You no longer explain your truth—because it's already evident

That's power.

Final Words from the Battlefield

You may not have chosen this war, but you've survived it with integrity. You've shown restraint in the face of rage. You've chosen evidence over emotion. You've stood in court alone and spoken calmly while she acted out a script.

And now?

Now you rise.

Now you move from defense to offense—not in aggression, but in truth.

You turn the tables every time you say:

> "No more lies. No more fear. No more control."

This book isn't your ending. It's your reentry. Into fatherhood, into manhood, into peace.

You've already won.

Author's Note

Author's Note

By Dr. Paul J. Peloquin, Sr., PhD

This book was born not in a classroom or a courtroom—but in the raw, private pain of personal experience.

I lived through the manipulation, the false accusations, the legal ambushes, and the endless cycle of gaslighting that too many men endure in silence. I wrote Courtroom Control for those who has been accused without evidence, ignored in front of judges, and alienated from their children—all while trying to hold onto their sanity.

If you are reading this, you've either survived the worst, or you're standing at its edge.

Let this be your reminder: you are not powerless. You are not crazy. You are not alone.

I offer these pages not just as a roadmap, but as a lifeline—from one survivor to another. May you use what's inside to protect your rights, defend your truth, and reclaim the life she tried to control.

You're stronger than you know.

— Dr. Paul J. Peloquin, Sr., PhD

Land O' Lakes, Florida

Back Cover Summary

Back Cover Text:

Courtroom Control

How Narcissists Weaponize the Legal System—And How to Fight Back

By Dr. Paul J. Peloquin, Sr., PhD

When a narcissist drags you into court, truth alone isn't enough.

With chilling precision, narcissistic partners can turn the legal system into a weapon—filing false accusations, manipulating custody, and playing the perfect victim to gain the upper hand. And too often, family courts can't see through the act.

In this groundbreaking book, Dr. Paul J. Peloquin, Sr.—a (Retired) psychologist and survivor of narcissistic abuse—exposes how narcissists exploit the legal process and shows you how to defend yourself at every stage. From divorce ambushes and restraining orders to co-parenting sabotage and courtroom strategies, Courtroom Control equips you with the tools, tactics, and confidence to protect your rights and your sanity.

This is more than a survival guide. It's a strategic war manual for men fighting in the shadow of legal and emotional abuse.

If you've been silenced, blamed, or blindsided—this book will help you rise, fight back, and win.

The End

Don't miss out!

Visit the website below and you can sign up to receive emails whenever Dr Paul J Peloquin Sr, PhD publishes a new book. There's no charge and no obligation.

https://books2read.com/r/B-A-URIYD-HOYKG

Connecting independent readers to independent writers.

About the Author

From Dr. Paul J. Peloquin Sr., PhD

This book was born out of silence.

Not the kind that comforts—but the kind that crushes. The kind that creeps into your life when you're too ashamed to speak. When you're too afraid to be disbelieved. When you've been told—over and over again—that your truth is not valid, your pain is not real, and your story is not worth telling.

I wrote Echoes of Control to prove that it is.

For years, I lived behind closed doors, enduring subtle manipulations and outright cruelty at the hands of a woman who wore a mask so well the world applauded while I quietly withered. I doubted myself. I questioned my worth. And I stayed longer than I should have—not out of weakness, but out of hope, loyalty, and the belief that love should be enough.

But some love isn't love. It's control. And some people don't want connection—they want submission.

This book is not a revenge story. It is a resurrection story.

Every chapter is a declaration: that men can be victims. That narcissistic abuse is real. That emotional trauma leaves scars just as deep as physical ones. And that no matter how long you've lived in darkness, the light is still yours to claim.

If you're reading this and you feel seen, I hope you also feel strengthened.

If you're reading this and you've survived something similar, I hope you feel validated.

And if you're still in the fog—I hope this book is your first glimpse of clarity.

You are not crazy.

You are not weak.

And you are not alone.

This is the NEW not the old normal...

– Dr. Paul J. Peloquin Sr., PhD